Preface

MathExpress - Speed Math Strategies series aims at developing new ways in acquiring mathematics skills for effective and enjoyable learning. It helps pupils improve speed and accuracy through the simple, fun-to-learn strategies introduced at different levels.

- ⮎ Level 1 - Addition & Subtraction Within 100
- ⮎ Level 2 - Addition & Subtraction Within 1000
- ⮎ Level 3 - More On Addition & Subtraction / Multiplication & Division
- ⮎ Level 4 - More On Multiplication / Decimals
- ⮎ Level 5 - Fractions / Checking Answers
- ⮎ Level 6 - Percentage / Other Topics

This series of books is recommended for both High and Low Achievers.

High Achievers - Challenging themselves to master speedy mental calculations, developing the ability to analyse, simplify and think laterally.

Low Achievers - Developing an interest for working, playing and experimenting with numbers as well as increasing their self-esteem. No more 'maths-phobia'!

The faster and easier method we use, the fewer mistakes we make!

Li Fanglan

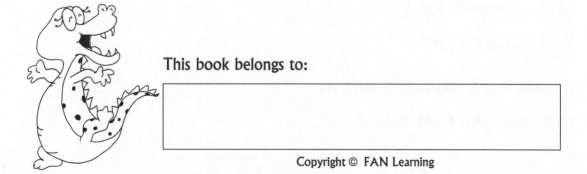

This book belongs to:

Contents

Express Strategy 1

Can you get the answers in 10 seconds?

(a)   56 + 9 = ?

(b)   136 + 8 = ?

Your Answer: (a) _____

(b) _____

Time Taken: _____ seconds

What is the value of <u>56</u> + <u>9</u>?

Solution:

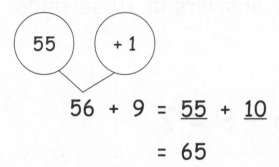

$$56 + 9 = \underline{55} + \underline{10}$$
$$= 65$$

9 and 1 make 10. Rewrite 56 as 55 + 1.

Add 1 to 9 to get 10 before adding 55.

Addition - Make 10

What is the value of <u>138 + 6</u>?

Solution:

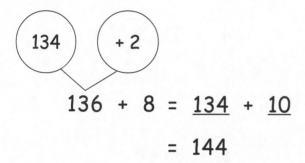

$$136 \; + \; 8 \; = \; \underline{134} \; + \; \underline{10}$$
$$= \; 144$$

8 and 2 make 10. Rewrite 136 as 134 + 2.

Add 2 to 8 to get 0 before adding 134.

Addition - Make 10

Do the sums using the strategy.

1.   34 + 9

2.   46 + 9

3.   65 + 9

4.   53 + 8

5.   75 + 8

6.   86 + 8

7.   125 + 9

8.   136 + 9

9.   143 + 8

10.   254 + 8

Solve the problems using the strategy.

1.   Darren has 37 guppies and 9 swordtails.
     How many fish does he have altogether?

2.   Jane has 46 comic books.
     Her mother buys her another 8 comic books.
     How many comic books does she have now?

Date: _____   Time Taken: _____   Marks:___/10

Do the following mentally. Write your answers in the boxes provided.

1.   35 + 9 = ⬚

2.   48 + 9 = ⬚

3.   66 + 9 = ⬚

4.   74 + 8 = ⬚

5.   83 + 8 = ⬚

6.   145 + 9 = ⬚

7.   136 + 8 = ⬚

8.   286 + 9 = ⬚

9.   There are 147 girls in a hall.
      There are 9 more boys than girls in the hall.
      How many boys are there in the hall?

      ⬚

Express Strategy 2

Can you get the answers in 10 seconds?

(a) 19 + 45 = ?

(b) 216 + 58 = ?

Your Answer: (a) _____

(b) _____

Time Taken: _____ seconds

What is the value of <u>19 + 45</u>?

Solution:

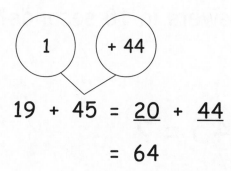

19 + 45 = <u>20</u> + <u>44</u>

= 64

19 and 1 make 20. Rewrite 45 as 1 + 44.

Add 1 to 19 to get 20 before adding 44.

Addition - Make Tens

What is the value of <u>216 + 58</u>?

Solution:

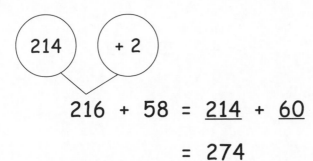

$$216 + 58 = \underline{214} + \underline{60}$$
$$= 274$$

58 and 2 make 60. Rewrite 216 as 214 + 2.

Add 2 to 58 to get 60 before adding 214.

Addition - Make Tens

Do the sums using the strategy.

1.   19 + 54

2.   65 + 19

3.   136 + 29

4.   155 + 39

5.   24 + 68

6.   58 + 33

7.   39 + 48

8.   123 + 38

9.   105 + 58

10.   215 + 47

Solve the problems using the strategy.

1. Joe collected 35 seashells.
   David collected 19 more seashells than Joe.
   How many seashells did David collect?

2. Rizal sold 125 curry puffs.
   Rani sold 28 curry puffs.
   How many curry puffs did they sell altogether?

Speed & Accuracy Test 2

Date: _____   Time Taken: _____   Marks:____/10

Do the following mentally. Write your answers in the boxes provided.

1. 47 + 19 = ☐

2. 39 + 33 = ☐

3. 138 + 29 = ☐

4. 123 + 39 = ☐

5. 38 + 34 = ☐

6. 26 + 68 = ☐

7. 143 + 48 = ☐

8. 214 + 78 = ☐

9. Henry received 126 stickers.
    May received 38 more stickers than Henry.
    How many stickers did May receive?

☐

Express Strategy 3

Can you get the answers in 10 seconds?

(a) 176 + 90 = ?

(b) 182 + 93 = ?

Your Answer: (a) _____

(b) _____

Time Taken: _____ seconds

What is the value of <u>176 + 90</u>?

Solution:

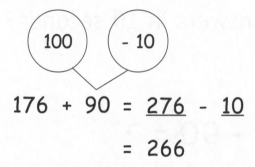

176 + 90 = <u>276</u> - <u>10</u>

= 266

90 is 10 less than 100.

Add 100 to 176 before subtracting 10.

Addition - Use 100

What is the value of <u>182 + 93</u>?

Solution:

$$182 + 93 \quad = \quad \underline{185} \; + \; \underline{90}$$

overhead: 100 \quad - 10

$$= \quad 285 - 10$$

$$= \quad 275$$

Since no regrouping is needed for adding the ones (2 + 3 = 5), rewrite 182 + 93 as 185 + 90.

90 is 10 less than 100. Add 100 to 185 before subtracting 10.

Addition - Use 100

Do the sums using the strategy.

1.   143 + 90

2.   156 + 90

3.   167 + 80

4.   235 + 80

5.   186 + 70

6.   283 + 81

7.   147 + 92

8.   163 + 84

9.   245 + 83

10.   274 + 75

Solve the problems using the strategy.

1. Alice has 137 paper clips.
    Danny has 80 more paper clips than Alice.
    How many paper clips does Danny have?

2. There are 145 goldfish in an aquarium.
    There are 82 guppies in the aquarium too.
    How many fish are there in the aquarium altogether?

Speed & Accuracy Test 3

Date: _____   Time Taken: _____   Marks:___/10

Do the following mentally. Write your answers in the boxes provided.

1.   154 + 90 = [   ]

2.   162 + 70 = [   ]

3.   231 + 80 = [   ]

4.   242 + 60 = [   ]

5.   164 + 71 = [   ]

6.   133 + 82 = [   ]

7.   326 + 92 = [   ]

8.   352 + 67 = [   ]

9.   There are 144 cars and 70 vans at a carpark.
     How many cars and vans are there at the carpark altogether?

[   ]

Express Strategy 4

Can you get the answers in 10 seconds?

(a)   362 + 180 = ?

(b)   273 + 184 = ?

Your Answer: (a) _____

(b) _____

Time Taken: _____ seconds

What is the value of <u>362 + 180</u>?

Solution:

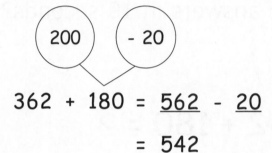

$$362 + 180 = \underline{562} - \underline{20}$$
$$= 542$$

180 is 20 less than 200.

Add 200 to 362 before subtracting 20.

Addition - Use Hundreds (1)

What is the value of 273 + 184?

Solution:

200   - 20

273 + 184 = 277 + 180

= 477 - 20

= 457

Since no regrouping is needed for adding the ones (3 + 4 = 7), rewrite 273 + 184 as 277 + 180.

180 is 20 less than 200. Add 200 to 277 before subtracting 20.

Addition - Use Hundreds (1)

Do the sums using the strategy.

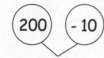

1.   168 + 190

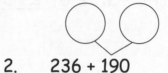

2.   236 + 190

3.   195 + 180

4.   283 + 180

5.   254 + 170

6.   144 + 271

7.   132 + 186

8.   185 + 153

9.   175 + 264

10.   187 + 342

Solve the problems using the strategy.

1.   There are 156 buttons in a box.
     Mrs Kumar puts in another 180 buttons.
     How many buttons are there in the box now?

2.   Jim collects 174 toy soldiers.
     Alvin collects 183 toy soldiers.
     How many toy soldiers do they collect altogether?

Date: _____   Time Taken: _____   Marks:____/10

Do the following mentally. Write your answers in the boxes provided.

1.   154 + 190 =

2.   256 + 180 =

3.   165 + 170 =

4.   283 + 180 =

5.   154 + 160 =

6.   145 + 192 =

7.   275 + 163 =

8.   584 + 233 =

9.   Mr Wee sold 186 eggs on Monday.
     He sold 230 eggs on Tuesday.
     How many eggs did he sell altogether in the two days?

Express Strategy 5

Can you get the answers in 10 seconds?

(a)   158 + 85 = ?

(b)   289 + 157 = ?

Your Answer: (a) _____

(b) _____

Time Taken: _____ seconds

What is the value of <u>158 + 85</u>?

Solution:

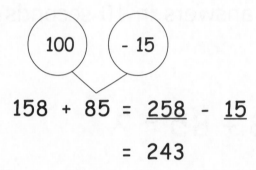

158 + 85 = <u>258</u> - <u>15</u>

= 243

85 is 15 less than 100.

Add 100 to 158 before subtracting 15.

Addition - Use Hundreds (2)

What is the value of <u>289 + 157</u>?

Solution:

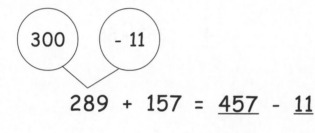

$$289 + 157 = \underline{457} - \underline{11}$$
$$= 446$$

289 is 11 less than 300.

Add 300 to 157 before subtracting 11.

Addition - Use Hundreds (2)

Worksheet 5A

Do the sums using the strategy.

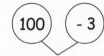

1. $135 + 97$

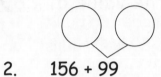

2. $156 + 99$

3. $147 + 89$

4. $263 + 88$

5. $245 + 86$

6. $138 + 75$

7. $139 + 186$

8. $188 + 126$

9. $175 + 158$

10. $187 + 347$

Solve the problems using the strategy.

1. Krishna made 145 buns.
    Raj made 89 more buns than Krishna.
    How many buns did Raj make?

2. A hawker bought 268 potatoes.
    He bought 175 more carrots than potatoes.
    How many carrots did he buy?

Date: _____   Time Taken: _____   Marks:____/10

Do the following mentally. Write your answers in the boxes provided.

1. 164 + 97 = [   ]

2. 133 + 89 = [   ]

3. 326 + 85 = [   ]

4. 134 + 69 = [   ]

5. 154 + 188 = [   ]

6. 145 + 195 = [   ]

7. 285 + 159 = [   ]

8. 187 + 247 = [   ]

9. Peter has 186 stamps.
    Nelson has 77 more stamps than Peter.
    How many stamps does Nelson have?

[   ]

Express Strategy 6

Can you get the answers in 10 seconds?

(a)   83 – 9 = ?

(b)   124 – 8 = ?

Your Answer: (a) _____

(b) _____

Time Taken: _____ seconds

What is the value of <u>83 - 9</u>?

Solution:

$$\overset{\overbrace{}}{\underset{- 10 \qquad + 1}{}}$$

83 - 9 = <u>73</u> + <u>1</u>

= 74

9 is 1 less than 10.

Subtract 10 from 83 before adding 1.

Subtraction - Use 10

What is the value of <u>124 - 8</u>?

Solution:

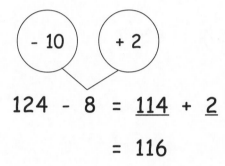

124 - 8 = <u>114</u> + <u>2</u>

= 116

8 is 2 less than 10.

Subtract 10 from 124 before adding 2.

Subtraction - Use 10

Worksheet 6A

Do the sums using the strategy.

1. 73 - 9

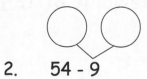

2. 54 - 9

3. 65 - 8

4. 82 - 7

5. 62 - 6

6. 121 - 9

7. 132 - 8

8. 140 - 9

9. 132 - 7

10. 151 - 6

Solve the problems using the strategy.

1.   74 children are dancing.
    9 of them are boys.
    How many girls are there?

2.   Linda and her mother folded 125 paper cranes altogether.
    Linda folded 8 paper cranes.
    How many paper cranes did her mother fold?

Speed & Accuracy Test 6

Date: _____   Time Taken: _____   Marks:___/10

Do the following mentally. Write your answers in the boxes provided.

1.   55 - 9 =

2.   47 - 8 =

3.   117 - 9 =

4.   93 - 7 =

5.   72 - 8 =

6.   136 - 9 =

7.   122 - 8 =

8.   111 - 6 =

9.   Krishna had 72 stickers.
      She gave her friend 7 stickers.
      How many stickers had she left?

Express Strategy 7

Can you get the answers in 10 seconds?

(a)   91 - 19 = ?

(b)   182 - 38 = ?

Your Answer: (a) _____

(b) _____

Time Taken: _____ seconds

What is the value of <u>91 - 19</u>?

Solution:

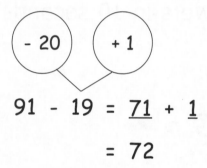

91 - 19 = <u>71</u> + <u>1</u>

= 72

19 is 1 less than 20.

Subtract 20 from 91 before adding 1.

Subtraction - Use Tens

38

What is the value of <u>182 - 38</u>?

Solution:

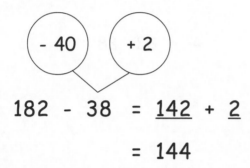

$$182 - 38 = \underline{142} + \underline{2}$$
$$= 144$$

38 is 2 less than 40.

Subtract 40 from 182 before adding 2.

Subtraction - Use Tens

Do the sums using the strategy.

   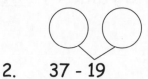

1.   43 – 19   2.   37 – 19

3.   54 – 29   4.   83 – 28

5.   71 – 37   6.   93 – 46

7.   132 – 18   8.   255 – 49

9.   180 – 57   10.   261 – 35

Solve the problems using the strategy.

1. There are 65 motorbikes and cars at a carpark altogether.
    28 of them are motorbikes.
    How many cars are there?

2. Daniel has 192 pigeons.
    47 of them are white and the rest are grey.
    How many grey pigeons does Daniel have?

Date: _____   Time Taken: _____   Marks: ___/10

Do the following mentally. Write your answers in the boxes provided.

1.   47 - 19 = ☐

2.   36 - 29 = ☐

3.   65 - 28 = ☐

4.   83 - 47 = ☐

5.   143 - 19 = ☐

6.   164 - 36 = ☐

7.   187 - 39 = ☐

8.   152 - 27 = ☐

9.   Ms Sue made 53 sticks of chicken and mutton satay altogether.
      She made 16 sticks of chicken satay.
      How many sticks of mutton satay did she make?

      ☐

Express Strategy 8

Can you get the answers in 10 seconds?

(a)   134 - 90 = ?

(b)   125 - 92 = ?

Your Answer: (a) _____

(b) _____

Time Taken: _____ seconds

What is the value of <u>134 - 90</u>?

Solution:

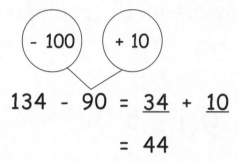

134 - 90 = <u>34</u> + <u>10</u>

= 44

90 is 10 less than 100.

Subtract 100 from 134 before adding 10.

Subtraction - Use 100

What is the value of <u>125 - 92</u>?

Solution:

$$125 - 92 = \underline{123} - \underline{90}$$
$$= 23 + 10$$
$$= 33$$

over the numbers: (- 100) (+ 10)

Since no regrouping is needed for subtracting the ones
(5 - 2 = 3), rewrite 125 - 92 as 123 - 90.
90 is 10 less than 100. Subtract 100 from 123 before adding 10.

Subtraction - Use 100

Worksheet 8A

Do the sums using the strategy.

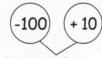
1. 123 - 90

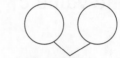
2. 145 - 90

3. 118 - 80

4. 154 - 80

5. 162 - 70

6. 146 - 92

7. 156 - 94

8. 274 - 83

9. 459 - 87

10. 537 - 64

Solve the problems using the strategy.

1.   Norla and Raj have 166 stamps altogether.
     Raj has 80 stamps.
     How many stamps does Norla have?

2.   James sold 245 concert tickets.
     Aileen sold 72 fewer concert tickets than James.
     How many concert tickets did Aileen sell?

Date: _____ Time Taken: _____ Marks:___/10

Do the following mentally. Write your answers in the boxes provided.

1.   131 - 90 = [ ]

2.   147 - 80 = [ ]

3.   115 - 70 = [ ]

4.   167 - 80 = [ ]

5.   173 - 91 = [ ]

6.   203 - 82 = [ ]

7.   166 - 73 = [ ]

8.   237 - 84 = [ ]

9.   Nury and her sister saved $136 altogether.
      Nury saved $90.
      How much money did her sister save?

      $ [ ]

Express Strategy 9

Can you get the answers in 10 seconds?

(a)   342 - 190 = ?

(b)   237 - 172 = ?

Your Answer: (a) _____

(b) _____

Time Taken: _____ seconds

What is the value of <u>342 - 190</u>?

Solution:

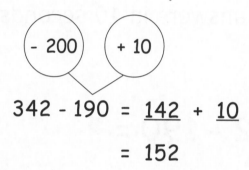

$$342 - 190 = \underline{142} + \underline{10}$$
$$= 152$$

190 is 10 less than 200.

Subtract 200 from 342 before adding 10.

Subtraction - Use Hundreds (1)

What is the value of <u>237 - 172</u>?

Solution:

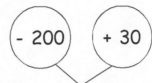

$$237 - 172 \;=\; \underline{235} \;-\; \underline{170}$$

$$=\; 35 \;+\; 30$$

$$=\; 65$$

Since no regrouping is needed for subtracting the ones
(7 - 2 = 5), rewrite 237 - 172 as 235 - 170.
170 is 30 less than 200. Subtract 200 from 235 before adding 30.

Subtraction - Use Hundreds (1)

Do the sums using the strategy.

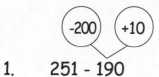

1.   251 - 190

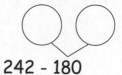

2.   242 - 180

3.   363 - 190

4.   356 - 170

5.   244 - 160

6.   218 - 195

7.   315 - 193

8.   347 - 185

9.   556 - 386

10.   659 - 281

Solve the problems using the strategy.

1. Bala has 263 rubber bands.
   Aisha has 180 fewer rubber bands than Bala.
   How many rubber bands does Aisha have?

2. There are 238 passengers on board a train.
   175 passengers are men.
   How many women are on board the train?

Speed & Accuracy Test 9

Do the following mentally. Write your answers in the boxes provided.

1.   247 - 190 =

2.   267 - 180 =

3.   314 - 170 =

4.   343 - 190 =

5.   411 - 270 =

6.   276 - 191 =

7.   335 - 172 =

8.   818 - 583 =

9.   Joe and May have 215 kiwi fruits altogether.
     Joe has 160 kiwi fruits.
     How many kiwi fruits does May have?

Express Strategy 10

Can you get the answers in 10 seconds?

(a) 253 - 88 = ?

(b) 743 - 588 = ?

Your Answer: (a) _____

(b) _____

Time Taken: _____ seconds

What is the value of <u>253 - 88</u>?

Solution:

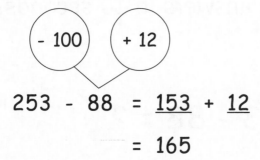

253 - 88 = <u>153</u> + <u>12</u>

= 165

88 is 12 less than 100.

Subtract 100 from 253 before adding 12 .

Subtraction - Use Hundreds (2)

What is the value of <u>743 - 588</u>?

Solution:

$$\overset{\displaystyle \left(-600\right)\ \ \left(+12\right)}{743 - 588} = \underline{143} + \underline{12}$$

$$= 155$$

588 is 12 less than 600.

Subtract 600 from 743 before adding 12.

Subtraction - Use Hundreds (2)

Do the sums using the strategy.

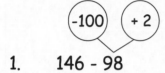

1. 146 - 98

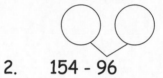

2. 154 - 96

3. 134 - 88

4. 103 - 85

5. 211 - 84

6. 281 - 195

7. 315 - 198

8. 334 - 189

9. 556 - 486

10. 653 - 477

Solve the problems using the strategy.

1. Philip saved $132. Dora saved $85.
    How much more money did Philip save than Dora?

2. A bakery made 530 cookies.
    284 cookies were sold.
    How many cookies were left?

Date: _____   Time Taken: _____   Marks:____/10

Do the following mentally. Write your answers in the boxes provided.

1.   173 - 98 =

2.   203 - 85 =

3.   166 - 77 =

4.   237 - 88 =

5.   266 - 198 =

6.   471 - 286 =

7.   535 - 379 =

8.   814 - 585 =

9.   Farhan and Nora scored 315 points in a game.
      Farhan scored 189 points.
      How many points did Nora score?

Express Strategy 11

Can you get the answers in 10 seconds?

(a)   100 - 47 = ?

(b)   700 - 368 = ?

Your Answer: (a) _____

(b) _____

Time Taken: _____ seconds

What is the value of <u>100 - 47</u>?

Solution:

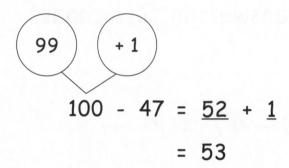

$$100 - 47 = \underline{52} + \underline{1}$$
$$= 53$$

Rewrite 100 as 99 + 1.

Subtract 47 from 99 before adding 1.

Subtraction - Take Away 1 From Hundreds

What is the value of <u>700 - 368</u>?

Solution:

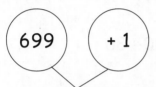

700 - 368 = <u>331</u> + <u>1</u>

= 332

Rewrite 700 as 699 + 1.

Subtract 368 from 699 before adding 1.

Subtraction - Take Away 1 From Hundreds

Worksheet 11A

Do the sums using the strategy.

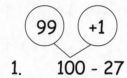

1. 100 - 27

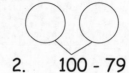

2. 100 - 79

3. 100 - 54

4. 100 - 36

5. 200 - 77

6. 200 - 78

7. 200 - 148

8. 300 - 147

9. 600 - 432

10. 1000 - 567

Solve the problems using the strategy.

1.   There were 100 balls in a box.
      Sulin took out 53 balls.
      How many balls were left in the box?

2.   Sam has 300 toy soldiers.
      Darren has 168 toy soldiers.
      How many more toy soldiers does Sam have than Darren?

Speed & Accuracy Test 11

Date: _____   Time Taken: _____   Marks:___/10

Do the following mentally. Write your answers in the boxes provided.

1.   100 - 23 = ☐   2.   100 - 56 = ☐

3.   100 - 47 = ☐   4.   200 - 29 = ☐

5.   1000 - 578 = ☐   6.   200 - 141 = ☐

7.   700 - 426 = ☐   8.   900 - 674 = ☐

9.   Mrs Cheng had $100. She spent $37 on a dictionary.
      How much money had she left?

$ ☐

Express Strategy 12

Can you get the answers in 10 seconds?

(a) 16 + 19 + 4 = ?

(b) 17 + 18 + 12 = ?

Your Answer: (a) _____

(b) _____

Time Taken: _____ seconds

What is the value of <u>16 + 19 + 4</u>?

Solution:

$$16 + 19 + 4 = \underline{20} + 19$$
$$= 39$$

16 and 4 make 20.

Add 16 to 4 before adding 19.

Addition - Pair Them Up

What is the value of <u>17 + 18 + 12</u>?

Solution:

$$17 + 18 + 12 = 17 + \underline{30}$$
$$= 47$$

18 and 12 make 30.

Add 18 and 12 before adding 17.

Addition - Pair Them Up

Do the sums using the strategy.

1. $\overparen{13 + 9} + 7$

2. $\overparen{8 + 17} + 12$

3. $19 + 15 + 11$

4. $14 + 19 + 6$

5. $17 + 8 + 13$

6. $14 + 15 + 16$

7. $15 + 18 + 12$

8. $13 + 9 + 11$

9. $19 + 15 + 15$

10. $24 + 17 + 23$

Solve the problems using the strategy.

1. A tailor used 14 red buttons, 9 blue buttons and 6 white buttons on a dress.
    How many buttons did she use altogether?

2. Jonathan cut a piece of wire into 3 pieces.
    The 1st piece was 8 cm long, the 2nd piece was 17 cm long and the 3rd piece was 12 cm long.
    Find the length of wire at first.

Speed & Accuracy Test 12

Date: _____   Time Taken: _____   Marks:___/10

Do the following mentally. Write your answers in the boxes provided.

1.   12 + 9 + 8 = ☐

2.   7 + 14 + 6 = ☐

3.   7 + 16 + 13 = ☐

4.   6 + 15 + 5 = ☐

5.   12 + 11 + 9 = ☐

6.   15 + 8 + 12 = ☐

7.   16 + 17 + 14 = ☐

8.   23 + 19 + 31 = ☐

9.   There are 8 red apples and 16 green apples in a basket.
     Mrs Raj puts in another 12 apples.
     How many apples are there in the basket now?

     ☐

Express Strategy 13

Can you get the answers in 10 seconds?

(a)   18 + 5 - 7 = ?

(b)   15 + 19 - 8 = ?

Your Answer: (a) _____

(b) _____

Time Taken: _____ seconds

What is the value of <u>18 + 5 - 7</u>?

Solution:

$$18 + 5 - 7 = \underline{11} + 5$$
$$= 16$$

Subtract 7 from 18 before adding 5.

Addition & Subtraction - Who Goes First

What is the value of 15 + 19 - 8?

Solution:

$$15 + 19 - 8 = 15 + \underline{11}$$
$$= 26$$

Subtract 8 from 19 before adding 15.

Addition & Subtraction - Who Goes First

Do the sums using the strategy.

1. $19 + 6 - 8$

2. $17 + 4 - 6$

3. $16 + 8 - 15$

4. $18 + 15 - 17$

5. $18 + 13 - 16$

6. $13 + 18 - 7$

7. $12 + 17 - 14$

8. $25 + 19 - 8$

9. $22 + 16 - 14$

10. $21 + 18 - 13$

Solve the problems using the strategy.

1. Jeremy had 17 red marbles and 5 green marbles.
    He gave some marbles to his brother.
    Then he had 14 marbles left.
    How many marbles did Jeremy give to his brother?

2. There were 16 boys and 27 girls in a class.
    23 pupils scored distinction in their Maths Test.
    How many pupils did not score distinction in the test?

Date: _____   Time Taken: _____   Marks:___/10

Do the following mentally. Write your answers in the boxes provided.

1.   17 + 8 - 13 =

2.   16 + 8 - 12 =

3.   18 + 7 - 16 =

4.   18 + 14 - 17 =

5.   14 + 17 - 16 =

6.   23 + 18 - 15 =

7.   14 + 19 - 16 =

8.   17 + 24 - 15 =

9.   There were 18 people in a bus.
      At a bus-stop, 9 people boarded the bus and 14 people alighted.
      How many people were in the bus finally?

Express Strategy 14

Can you get the answers in 10 seconds?

(a)   14 + 9 – 15 = ?

(b)   16 + 9 – 18 = ?

Your Answer: (a) _____

(b) _____

Time Taken: _____ seconds

What is the value of <u>14 + 9 - 15</u>?

Solution:

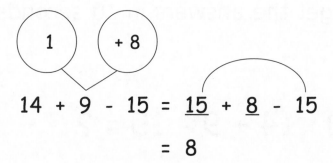

$$14 + 9 - 15 = \underline{15} + \underline{8} - 15$$

$$= 8$$

14 is 1 less than 15.

Rewrite 9 as 1 + 8. Add 1 to 14 to get 15.

Subtract 15 from 15, leaving 8 as the answer.

Addition & Subtraction - Tapping On Others

What is the value of <u>16 + 9 - 18</u>?

Solution:

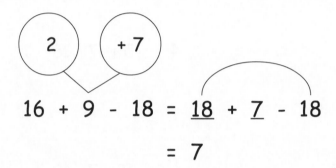

16 + 9 - 18 = <u>18</u> + <u>7</u> - 18

= 7

16 is 2 less than 18.

Rewrite 9 as 2 + 7. Add 2 to 16 to get 18.

Subtract 18 from 18, leaving 7 as the answer.

Addition & Subtraction - Tapping On Others

Worksheet 14A

Do the sums using the strategy.

1. 16 + 8 - 17

2. 17 + 9 - 18

3. 15 + 6 - 7

4. 5 + 17 - 18

5. 7 + 14 - 15

6. 18 + 7 - 19

7. 15 + 8 - 17

8. 13 + 16 - 18

9. 16 + 17 - 19

10. 16 + 15 - 19

Solve the problems using the strategy.

1. Jeremy had 8 red pens and 14 blue pens.
    He gave 15 pens to his friend.
    How many pens had he left?

2. There are 14 boys and 8 girls at a party.
    16 of them wear spectacles.
    How many children do not wear spectacles?

Speed & Accuracy Test 14

Date: _____   Time Taken: _____   Marks:___/10

Do the following mentally. Write your answers in the boxes provided.

1.   17 + 6 - 19 =

2.   16 + 8 - 9 =

3.   12 + 15 - 17 =

4.   17 + 9 - 18 =

5.   14 + 8 - 15 =

6.   7 + 16 - 18 =

7.   9 + 14 - 17 =

8.   23 + 18 - 26 =

9.   Danny saved $16 last week and $9 this week.
      He spent $17 on a pair of shoes.
      How much money had he left?

      $

Do the following mentally. Write your answers in the boxes provided.

1. 125 + 9 =

2. 39 + 48 =

3. 163 + 84 =

4. 185 + 153 =

5. 188 + 126 =

6. 140 - 9 =

7. 255 - 49 =

8. 156 - 94 =

9. 347 - 185 =

10. 334 - 189 =

11. 300 - 147 =

12. 13 + 9 + 11 =

13. 25 + 19 - 8 =

14. 15 + 8 - 17 =

Date: _____   Time Taken: _____   Marks:____/28

Do the following mentally. Write your answers in the boxes provided.

1. $136 + 9 =$ ☐

2. $123 + 38 =$ ☐

3. $147 + 92 =$ ☐

4. $132 + 186 =$ ☐

5. $139 + 186 =$ ☐

6. $132 - 8 =$ ☐

7. $132 - 18 =$ ☐

8. $274 - 83 =$ ☐

9. $315 - 193 =$ ☐

10. $315 - 198 =$ ☐

11. $200 - 148 =$ ☐

12. $15 + 18 + 12 =$ ☐

13. $12 + 17 - 14 =$ ☐

14. $13 + 16 - 18 =$ ☐

Answer Key And Detailed Solutions

Worksheet 1A

1. 34 + 9
= 33 + 10
= 43

2. 46 + 9
= 45 + 10
= 55

3. 65 + 9
= 64 + 10
= 74

4. 53 + 8
= 51 + 10
= 61

5. 75 + 8
= 73 + 10
= 83

6. 86 + 8
= 84 + 10
= 94

7. 125 + 9
= 124 + 10
= 134

8. 136 + 9
= 135 + 10
= 145

9. 143 + 8
= 141 + 10
= 151

10. 254 + 8
= 252 + 10
= 262

Worksheet 1B

1. 37 + 9
= 36 + 10
= 46

2. 46 + 8
= 44 + 10
= 54

Speed & Accuracy Test 1

1. 35 + 9
= 34 + 10
= 44

2. 48 + 9
= 47 + 10
= 57

3. 66 + 9
= 65 + 10
= 75

4. 74 + 8
= 72 + 10
= 82

5. 83 + 8
= 81 + 10
= 91

6. 145 + 9
= 144 + 10
= 154

7. 136 + 8
= 134 + 10
= 144

8. 286 + 9
= 285 + 10
= 295

9. 147 + 9
= 146 + 10
= 156

Worksheet 2A

1. 19 + 54
   = 20 + 53
   = 73

2. 65 + 19
   = 64 + 20
   = 84

3. 136 + 29
   = 135 + 30
   = 165

4. 155 + 39
   = 154 + 40
   = 194

5. 24 + 68
   = 22 + 70
   = 92

6. 58 + 33
   = 60 + 31
   = 91

7. 39 + 48
   = 40 + 47
   = 87

8. 123 + 38
   = 121 + 40
   = 161

9. 105 + 58
   = 103 + 60
   = 163

10. 215 + 47
    = 212 + 50
    = 262

Worksheet 2B

1. 35 + 19
   = 34 + 20
   = 54

2. 125 + 28
   = 123 + 30
   = 153

Speed & Accuracy Test 2

1. 47 + 19
   = 46 + 20
   = 66

2. 39 + 33
   = 40 + 32
   = 72

3. 138 + 29
   = 137 + 30
   = 167

4. 123 + 39
   = 122 + 40
   = 162

5. 38 + 34
   = 40 + 32
   = 72

6. 26 + 68
   = 24 + 70
   = 94

7. 143 + 48
   = 141 + 50
   = 191

8. 214 + 78
   = 212 + 80
   = 292

9. 126 + 38
   = 124 + 40
   = 164

Worksheet 3A

1.   143 + 90
    = 243 - 10
    = 233

2.   156 + 90
    = 256 - 10
    = 246

3.   167 + 80
    = 267 - 20
    = 247

4.   235 + 80
    = 335 - 20
    = 315

5.   186 + 70
    = 286 - 30
    = 256

6.   283 + 81
    = 284 + 80
    = 384 - 20
    = 364

7.   147 + 92
    = 149 + 90
    = 249 - 10
    = 239

8.   163 + 84
    = 167 + 80
    = 267 - 20
    = 247

9.   245 + 83
    = 248 + 80
    = 348 - 20
    = 328

10.   274 + 75
    = 279 + 70
    = 379 - 30
    = 349

Worksheet 3B

1.   137 + 80
    = 237 - 20
    = 217

2.   145 + 82
    = 147 + 80
    = 247 - 20
    = 227

Speed & Accuracy Test 3

1.   154 + 90
    = 254 - 10
    = 244

2.   162 + 70
    = 262 - 30
    = 232

3.   231 + 80
    = 331 - 20
    = 311

4.   242 + 60
    = 342 - 40
    = 302

5.   164 + 71
    = 165 + 70
    = 265 - 30
    = 235

6.   133 + 82
    = 135 + 80
    = 235 - 20
    = 215

7.   326 + 92
    = 328 + 90
    = 428 - 10
    = 418

8.   352 + 67
    = 359 + 60
    = 459 - 40
    = 419

9.   144 + 70
    = 244 - 30
    = 214

Worksheet 4A

1. 168 + 190
= 368 - 10
= 358

2. 236 + 190
= 436 - 10
= 426

3. 195 + 180
= 395 - 20
= 375

4. 283 + 180
= 483 - 20
= 463

5. 254 + 170
= 454 - 30
= 424

6. 144 + 271
= 145 + 270
= 445 - 30
= 415

7. 132 + 186
= 138 + 180
= 338 - 20
= 318

8. 185 + 153
= 188 + 150
= 388 - 50
= 338

9. 175 + 264
= 179 + 260
= 479 - 40
= 439

10. 187 + 342
= 189 + 340
= 589 - 60
= 529

Worksheet 4B

1. 156 + 180
= 356 - 20
= 336

2. 174 + 183
= 177 + 180
= 377 - 20
= 357

Speed & Accuracy Test 4

1. 154 + 190
= 354 - 10
= 344

2. 256 + 180
= 456 - 20
= 436

3. 165 + 170
= 365 - 30
= 335

4. 283 + 180
= 483 - 20
= 463

5. 154 + 160
= 354 - 40
= 314

6. 145 + 192
= 147 + 190
= 347 - 10
= 337

7. 275 + 163
= 278 + 160
= 478 - 40
= 438

8. 584 + 233
= 587 + 230
= 887 - 70
= 817

9. 186 + 230
= 486 - 70
= 416

Worksheet 5A

1. 135 + 97
   = 235 - 3
   = 232

2. 156 + 99
   = 256 - 1
   = 255

3. 147 + 89
   = 247 - 11
   = 236

4. 263 + 88
   = 363 - 12
   = 351

5. 245 + 86
   = 345 - 14
   = 331

6. 138 + 75
   = 238 - 25
   = 213

7. 139 + 186
   = 339 - 14
   = 325

8. 188 + 126
   = 326 - 12
   = 314

9. 175 + 158
   = 358 - 25
   = 333

10. 187 + 347
    = 547 - 13
    = 534

Worksheet 5B

1. 145 + 89
   = 245 - 11
   = 234

2. 268 + 175
   = 468 - 25
   = 443

Speed & Accuracy Test 5

1. 164 + 97
   = 264 - 3
   = 261

2. 133 + 89
   = 233 - 11
   = 222

3. 326 + 85
   = 426 - 15
   = 411

4. 134 + 69
   = 234 - 31
   = 203

5. 154 + 188
   = 354 - 12
   = 342

6. 145 + 195
   = 345 - 5
   = 340

7. 285 + 159
   = 459 - 15
   = 444

8. 187 + 247
   = 447 - 13
   = 434

9. 186 + 77
   = 286 - 23
   = 263

Worksheet 6A

1. 73 - 9
   = 63 + 1
   = 64

2. 54 - 9
   = 44 + 1
   = 45

3. 65 - 8
   = 55 + 2
   = 57

4. 82 - 7
   = 72 + 3
   = 75

5. 62 - 6
   = 52 + 4
   = 56

6. 121 - 9
   = 111 + 1
   = 112

7. 132 - 8
   = 122 + 2
   = 124

8. 140 - 9
   = 130 + 1
   = 131

9. 132 - 7
   = 122 + 3
   = 125

10. 151 - 6
    = 141 + 4
    = 145

Worksheet 6B

1. 74 - 9
   = 64 + 1
   = 65

2. 125 - 8
   = 115 + 2
   = 117

Speed & Accuracy Test 6

1. 55 - 9
   = 45 + 1
   = 46

2. 47 - 8
   = 37 + 2
   = 39

3. 117 - 9
   = 107 + 1
   = 108

4. 93 - 7
   = 83 + 3
   = 86

5. 72 - 8
   = 62 + 2
   = 64

6. 136 - 9
   = 126 + 1
   = 127

7. 122 - 8
   = 112 + 2
   = 114

8. 111 - 6
   = 101 + 4
   = 105

9. 72 - 7
   = 62 + 3
   = 65

Worksheet 7A

1. 43 - 19
= 23 + 1
= 24

2. 37 - 19
= 17 + 1
= 18

3. 54 - 29
= 24 + 1
= 25

4. 83 - 28
= 53 + 2
= 55

5. 71 - 37
= 31 + 3
= 34

6. 93 - 46
= 43 + 4
= 47

7. 132 - 18
= 112 + 2
= 114

8. 255 - 49
= 205 + 1
= 206

9. 180 - 57
= 120 + 3
= 123

10. 261 - 35
= 221 + 5
= 226

Worksheet 7B

1. 65 - 28
= 35 + 2
= 37

2. 192 - 47
= 142 + 3
= 145

Speed & Accuracy Test 7

1. 47 - 19
= 27 + 1
= 28

2. 36 - 29
= 6 + 1
= 7

3. 65 - 28
= 35 + 2
= 37

4. 83 - 47
= 33 + 3
= 36

5. 143 - 19
= 123 + 1
= 124

6. 164 - 36
= 124 + 4
= 128

7. 187 - 39
= 147 + 1
= 148

8. 152 - 27
= 122 + 3
= 125

9. 53 - 16
= 33 + 4
= 37

Worksheet 8A

1. 123 - 90
    = 23 + 10
    = 33

2. 145 - 90
    = 45 + 10
    = 55

3. 118 - 80
    = 18 + 20
    = 38

4. 154 - 80
    = 54 + 20
    = 74

5. 162 - 70
    = 62 + 30
    = 92

6. 146 - 92
    = 144 - 90
    = 44 + 10
    = 54

7. 156 - 94
    = 152 - 90
    = 52 + 10
    = 62

8. 274 - 83
    = 271 - 80
    = 171 + 20
    = 191

9. 459 - 87
    = 452 - 80
    = 352 + 20
    = 372

10. 537 - 64
    = 533 - 60
    = 433 + 40
    = 473

Worksheet 8B

1. 166 - 80
    = 66 + 20
    = 86

2. 245 - 72
    = 243 - 70
    = 143 + 30
    = 173

Speed & Accuracy Test 8

1. 131 - 90
    = 31 + 10
    = 41

2. 147 - 80
    = 47 + 20
    = 67

3. 115 - 70
    = 15 + 30
    = 45

4. 167 - 80
    = 67 + 20
    = 87

5. 173 - 91
    = 172 - 90
    = 72 + 10
    = 82

6. 203 - 82
    = 201 - 80
    = 101 + 20
    = 121

7. 166 - 73
    = 163 - 70
    = 63 + 30
    = 93

8. 237 - 84
    = 233 - 80
    = 133 + 20 = 153

9. 136 - 90
    = 36 + 10
    = $46

Worksheet 9A

1. 251 - 190
    = 51 + 10
    = 61

2. 242 - 180
    = 42 + 20
    = 62

3. 363 - 190
    = 163 + 10
    = 173

4. 356 - 170
    = 156 + 30
    = 186

5. 244 - 160
    = 44 + 40
    = 84

6. 218 - 195
    = 213 - 190
    = 13 + 10
    = 23

7. 315 - 193
    = 312 - 190
    = 112 + 10
    = 122

8. 347 - 185
    = 342 - 180
    = 142 + 20
    = 162

9. 556 - 386
    = 550 - 380
    = 150 + 20
    = 170

10. 659 - 281
    = 658 - 280
    = 358 + 20
    = 378

Worksheet 9B

1. 263 - 180
    = 63 + 20
    = 83

2. 238 - 175
    = 233 - 170
    = 33 + 30
    = 63

Speed & Accuracy Test 9

1. 247 - 190
    = 47 + 10
    = 57

2. 267 - 180
    = 67 + 20
    = 87

3. 314 - 170
    = 114 + 30
    = 144

4. 343 - 190
    = 143 + 10
    = 153

5. 411 - 270
    = 111 + 30
    = 141

6. 276 - 191
    = 275 - 190
    = 75 + 10
    = 85

7. 335 - 172
    = 333 - 170
    = 133 + 30
    = 163

8. 818 - 583
    = 815 - 580
    = 215 + 20 = 235

9. 215 - 160
    = 15 + 40
    = 55

Worksheet 10A

1. 146 - 98
= 46 + 2
= 48

2. 154 - 96
= 54 + 4
= 58

3. 134 - 88
= 34 + 12
= 46

4. 103 - 85
= 3 + 15
= 18

5. 211 - 84
= 111 + 16
= 127

6. 281 - 195
= 81 + 5
= 86

7. 315 - 198
= 115 + 2
= 117

8. 334 - 189
= 134 + 11
= 145

9. 556 - 486
= 56 + 14
= 70

10. 653 - 477
= 153 + 23
= 176

Worksheet 10B

1. 132 - 85
= 32 + 15
= $47

2. 530 - 284
= 230 + 16
= 246

Speed & Accuracy Test 10

1. 173 - 98
= 73 + 2
= 75

2. 203 - 85
= 103 + 15
= 118

3. 166 - 77
= 66 + 23
= 89

4. 237 - 88
= 137 + 12
= 149

5. 266 - 198
= 66 + 2
= 68

6. 471 - 286
= 171 + 14
= 185

7. 535 - 379
= 135 + 21
= 156

8. 814 - 585
= 214 + 15
= 229

9. 315 - 189
= 115 + 11
= 126

Worksheet 11A

1. 100 - 27
   = 99 - 27 + 1
   = 73

2. 100 - 79
   = 99 - 79 + 1
   = 21

3. 100 - 54
   = 99 - 54 + 1
   = 46

4. 100 - 36
   = 99 - 36 + 1
   = 64

5. 200 - 77
   = 199 - 77 + 1
   = 123

6. 200 - 78
   = 199 - 78 + 1
   = 122

7. 200 - 148
   = 199 - 148 + 1
   = 52

8. 300 - 147
   = 299 - 147 + 1
   = 153

9. 600 - 432
   = 599 - 432 + 1
   = 168

10. 1000 - 567
    = 999 - 567 + 1
    = 433

Worksheet 11B

1. 100 - 53
   = 99 - 53 + 1
   = 47

2. 300 - 168
   = 299 - 168 + 1
   = 132

Speed & Accuracy Test 11

1. 100 - 23
   = 99 - 23 + 1
   = 77

2. 100 - 56
   = 99 - 56 + 1
   = 44

3. 100 - 47
   = 99 - 47 + 1
   = 53

4. 200 - 29
   = 199 - 29 + 1
   = 171

5. 1000 - 578
   = 999 - 578 + 1
   = 422

6. 200 - 141
   = 199 - 141 + 1
   = 59

7. 700 - 426
   = 699 - 426 + 1
   = 274

8. 900 - 674
   = 899 - 674 + 1
   = 226

9. 100 - 37
   = 99 - 37 + 1
   = $63

Worksheet 12A

1. $13 + 9 + 7$
   $= 20 + 9$
   $= 29$

2. $8 + 17 + 12$
   $= 20 + 17$
   $= 37$

3. $19 + 15 + 11$
   $= 30 + 15$
   $= 45$

4. $14 + 19 + 6$
   $= 20 + 19$
   $= 39$

5. $17 + 8 + 13$
   $= 30 + 8$
   $= 38$

6. $14 + 15 + 16$
   $= 30 + 15$
   $= 45$

7. $15 + 18 + 12$
   $= 15 + 30$
   $= 45$

8. $13 + 9 + 11$
   $= 13 + 20$
   $= 33$

9. $19 + 15 + 15$
   $= 19 + 30$
   $= 49$

10. $24 + 17 + 23$
    $= 24 + 40$
    $= 64$

Worksheet 12B

1. $14 + 9 + 6$
   $= 20 + 9$
   $= 29$

2. $8 + 17 + 12$
   $= 20 + 17$
   $= 37$ cm

Speed & Accuracy Test 12

1. $12 + 9 + 8$
   $= 20 + 9$
   $= 29$

2. $7 + 14 + 6$
   $= 7 + 20$
   $= 27$

3. $7 + 16 + 13$
   $= 20 + 16$
   $= 36$

4. $6 + 15 + 5$
   $= 6 + 20$
   $= 26$

5. $12 + 11 + 9$
   $= 12 + 20$
   $= 32$

6. $15 + 8 + 12$
   $= 15 + 20$
   $= 35$

7. $16 + 17 + 14$
   $= 30 + 17$
   $= 47$

8. $23 + 19 + 31$
   $= 23 + 50$
   $= 73$

9. $8 + 16 + 12$
   $= 20 + 16$
   $= 36$

Worksheet 13A

1. $19 + 6 - 8$
$= 11 + 6$
$= 17$

2. $17 + 4 - 6$
$= 11 + 4$
$= 15$

3. $16 + 8 - 15$
$= 1 + 8$
$= 9$

4. $18 + 15 - 17$
$= 1 + 15$
$= 16$

5. $18 + 13 - 16$
$= 2 + 13$
$= 15$

6. $13 + 18 - 7$
$= 13 + 11$
$= 24$

7. $12 + 17 - 14$
$= 12 + 3$
$= 15$

8. $25 + 19 - 8$
$= 25 + 11$
$= 36$

9. $22 + 16 - 14$
$= 22 + 2$
$= 24$

10. $21 + 18 - 13$
$= 21 + 5$
$= 26$

Worksheet 13B

1. $17 + 5 - 14$
$= 3 + 5$
$= 8$

2. $16 + 27 - 23$
$= 16 + 4$
$= 20$

Speed & Accuracy Test 13

1. $17 + 8 - 13$
$= 4 + 8$
$= 12$

2. $16 + 8 - 12$
$= 4 + 8$
$= 12$

3. $18 + 7 - 16$
$= 2 + 7$
$= 9$

4. $18 + 14 - 17$
$= 1 + 14$
$= 15$

5. $14 + 17 - 16$
$= 14 + 1$
$= 15$

6. $23 + 18 - 15$
$= 23 + 3$
$= 26$

7. $14 + 19 - 16$
$= 14 + 3$
$= 17$

8. $17 + 24 - 15$
$= 2 + 24$
$= 26$

9. $18 + 9 - 14$
$= 4 + 9$
$= 13$

Worksheet 14A

1. $16 + 8 - 17$
   $= 17 + 7 - 17$
   $= 7$

2. $17 + 9 - 18$
   $= 18 + 8 - 18$
   $= 8$

3. $15 + 6 - 7$
   $= 14 + 7 - 7$
   $= 14$

4. $5 + 17 - 18$
   $= 4 + 18 - 18$
   $= 4$

5. $7 + 14 - 15$
   $= 6 + 15 - 15$
   $= 6$

6. $18 + 7 - 19$
   $= 19 + 6 - 19$
   $= 6$

7. $15 + 8 - 17$
   $= 17 + 6 - 17$
   $= 6$

8. $13 + 16 - 18$
   $= 11 + 18 - 18$
   $= 11$

9. $16 + 17 - 19$
   $= 14 + 19 - 19$
   $= 14$

10. $16 + 15 - 19$
    $= 19 + 12 - 19$
    $= 12$

Worksheet 14B

1. $8 + 14 - 15$
   $= 7 + 15 - 15$
   $= 7$

2. $14 + 8 - 16$
   $= 16 + 6 - 16$
   $= 6$

Speed & Accuracy Test 14

1. $17 + 6 - 19$
   $= 19 + 4 - 19$
   $= 4$

2. $16 + 8 - 9$
   $= 15 + 9 - 9$
   $= 15$

3. $12 + 15 - 17$
   $= 10 + 17 - 17$
   $= 10$

4. $17 + 9 - 18$
   $= 18 + 8 - 18$
   $= 8$

5. $14 + 8 - 15$
   $= 15 + 7 - 15$
   $= 7$

6. $7 + 16 - 18$
   $= 5 + 18 - 18$
   $= 5$

7. $9 + 14 - 17$
   $= 6 + 17 - 17$
   $= 6$

8. $23 + 18 - 26$
   $= 26 + 15 - 26$
   $= 15$

9. $16 + 9 - 17$
   $= 17 + 8 - 17$
   $= \$8$

Diagnostic Test 1

1. $125 + 9 = 124 + 10 = 134$

2. $39 + 48 = 40 + 47 = 87$

3. $163 + 84$
   $= 167 + 80$
   $= 267 - 20$
   $= 247$

4. $185 + 153$
   $= 188 + 150$
   $= 388 - 50$
   $= 338$

5. $188 + 126 = 326 - 12 = 314$

6. $140 - 9 = 130 + 1 = 131$

7. $255 - 49 = 205 + 1 = 206$

8. $156 - 94$
   $= 152 - 90$
   $= 52 + 10$
   $= 62$

9. $347 - 185$
   $= 342 - 180$
   $= 142 + 20$
   $= 162$

10. $334 - 189 = 134 + 11 = 145$

11. $300 - 147$
    $= 299 - 147 + 1$
    $= 153$

12. $13 + 9 + 11 = 13 + 20 = 33$

13. $25 + 19 - 8 = 25 + 11 = 36$

14. $15 + 8 - 17$
    $= 17 + 6 - 17$
    $= 6$

Diagnostic Test 2

1. $136 + 9 = 135 + 10 = 145$

2. $123 + 38 = 121 + 40 = 161$

3. $147 + 92$
   $= 149 + 90$
   $= 249 - 10$
   $= 239$

4. $132 + 186$
   $= 138 + 180$
   $= 338 - 20$
   $= 318$

5. $139 + 186 = 339 - 14 = 325$

6. $132 - 8 = 122 + 2 = 124$

7. $132 - 18 = 112 + 2 = 114$

8. $274 - 83$
   $= 271 - 80$
   $= 171 + 20$
   $= 191$

9. $315 - 193$
   $= 312 - 190$
   $= 112 + 10$
   $= 122$

10. $315 - 198 = 115 + 2 = 117$

11. $200 - 148$
    $= 199 - 148 + 1$
    $= 52$

12. $15 + 18 + 12 = 15 + 30 = 45$

13. $12 + 17 - 14 = 12 + 3 = 15$

14. $13 + 16 - 18$
    $= 11 + 18 - 18$
    $= 11$

Singapore Math Specialist

SUCCESS IN MATH

THE BEST COMBINATION EVER

A   B   C   D

'TOP 10 MATHS' WRITER
Li Fanglan
(B.Sc., Dip in Ed.)

4 books are included:

A. Topical Revisions

B. Problem Solving Strategies

C. Speed Maths Strategies

D. Test Papers

SUCCESS

FAN-Math Publications
Quality Mathematics Books Not To Be Missed!